Ou Fantastic World

Contents

Written by Jan Burchett and Sara Vogler
Illustrated by Yi Jong

Collins

Stunning sights occur each day on Earth. Some happen right outside your house. Some you may never see.

Let's take a look at some of the most astonishing sights.

Superb rainbows

In wet weather, rainbows can form when the sun shines on rain.

Top tip: Keep your back to the sun when searching for a rainbow.

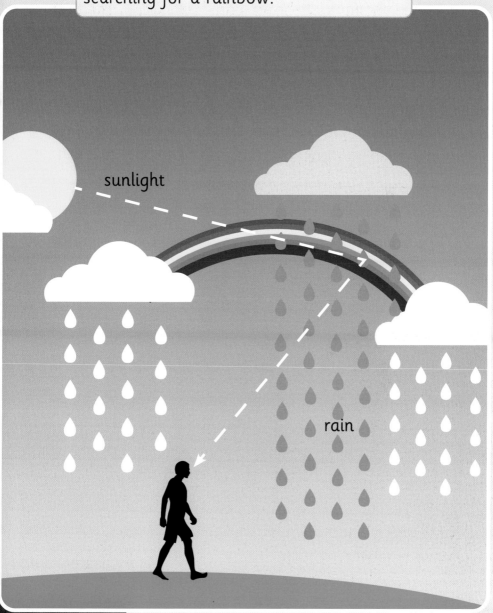

Have you heard of a **fogbow**?

Have you heard of a **snowbow**?

Or a **moonbow**?

How do you think they form?

Myth: An Irish myth says there's gold hidden deep underground at a rainbow's end.

But it's not worth looking as you can never reach the end of a rainbow!

Volcanic flames

What is this?

Myth: When the **blacksmith** god Vulcan got cross, he beat his **anvil** with a hammer. Sparks and rocks exploded all over the earth.

In real life, volcanic flames can be red or blue.

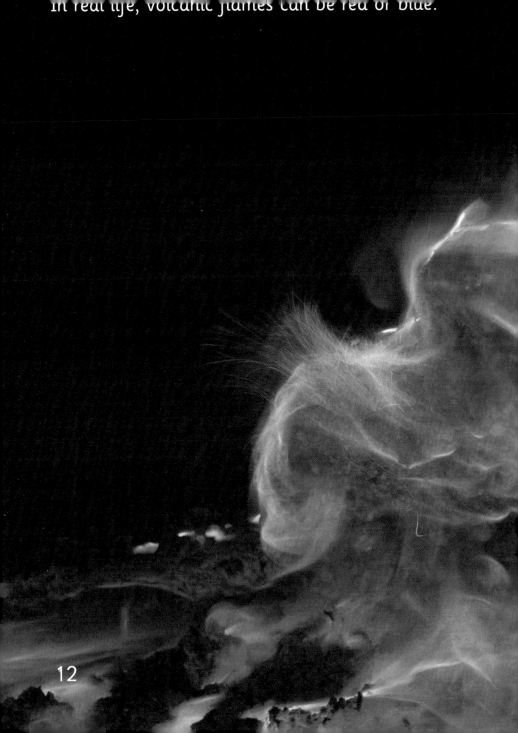

The flames can turn blue when gas inside the earth mixes with the air outside.

Some gas turns to liquid and spreads down the slopes like a boiling blue river.

It glows in the dark so it's worth seeing it at night.

Northern Lights

The Northern Lights form when the sun's wind hits Earth's **magnetic field**.

It's the best light show in the world!

The North and South Poles work as magnets.

The lights are much brighter at the North and South Poles so it's best to see them there.

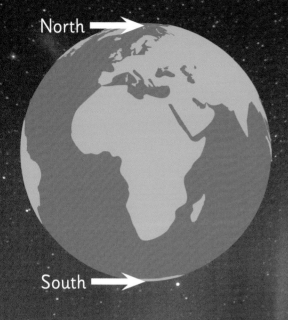

North ➝

South ➝

The lights stir and twirl overhead and form superb patterns.

Inuit myth: The lights are spirits playing football.

Finnish myth: The lights are foxes running over the Arctic snow.

Thunderstorms

This is a thundercloud. What would you do if this cloud was swirling overhead?

Top tip: Do not go outside.
Shelter in a house or car instead.

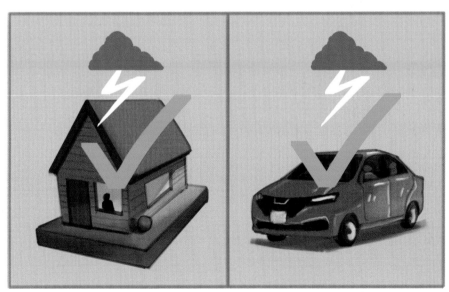

Lightning is five times hotter than the sun!

Ball lightning zooms round in a thunderstorm.

It makes a hissing sound
and has a bad smell.
It can smash windows!

Thundersnow has thunder and lightning but snow and hail **pelt** the earth instead of rain.

Myth: People said that thunder was the gods throwing **thunderbolts** down to Earth.

Glossary

anvil a strong block with a flat top. Heated metal objects are hammered into shapes on it.

blacksmith a person working on an anvil

Finnish from Finland

fogbow formed when the sun shines on fog

Inuit a member of a group of people living in the Arctic

magnetic field how far from a magnet its power works

moonbow formed when the moon shines on rain

myth old tale that is handed down from the past. Myths are stories and not facts.

pelt hit over and over

snowbow formed when the sun shines on falling snow

thunderbolts bolts of lightning shooting down to Earth

Index

Our world

What new facts did you learn from this book?

What would you tell a friend to do in this weather?

❂ **After reading** ❂

Letters and Sounds: Phase 5

Word count: 374

Focus phonemes: /ai/ ay, a-e, ey /ee/ ie, ea /igh/ i-e, i /oa/ o, ow, o-e /oo/ ue, ou, u, oul /ar/ a /ow/ ou /or/ al, our /ur/ ear, or, ir /e/ ea /i/ y

Common exception words: of, to, the, are, he, said, have, do, when, what, house, says, our, friend, there, was, some, people, be, into

Curriculum links: Geography: Human and physical geography

National Curriculum learning objectives: Reading/word reading: apply phonic knowledge and skills as the route to decode words; read accurately by blending sounds in unfamiliar words containing GPCs that have been taught; read words with contractions, and understand that the apostrophe represents the omitted letter(s); Reading/comprehension (KS2): understand what they read, in books they can read independently, by checking that the text makes sense to them, discussing their understanding and explaining the meaning of words in context; identifying main ideas drawn from more than one paragraph and summarising these

Developing fluency

- Take turns to read a page, demonstrating reading with expression and pausing for commas, full stops and colons.

Phonic practice

- Turn to page 19 and challenge your child to spot the words containing the /ur/ sound. (*twirl, stir, superb, patterns*) What letters make the /ur/ sound in these words? (*ir, er*)
- Ask your child to identify the letters that make the /ur/ sound in the following words, as they sound out and blend:
  learn (*ear*)   worth (*or*)   Earth (*ear*)   work (*or*)   swirling (*ir*)

Extending vocabulary

- Look together at page 8 and point to **there's**. Discuss what letter the apostrophe shows is missing. (*i – there is*)
- Challenge your child to shorten the following phrases with an apostrophe:
  she is (*she's*)   we will (*we'll*)   they are (*they're*)   we are (*we're*)